AI Audit Defense & Risk Reduction

How Businesses Avoid Costly IRS Investigations

By Joe Correa

Published by Live Stronger Faster

This book is for educational and informational purposes only. The author and publisher are not engaged in rendering legal, financial, tax, or other professional advice. Readers should consult a qualified professional before making any financial decisions.

First Edition

Table of Contents

Introduction

In the modern economy the greatest tax threat facing a business is no longer simply how much tax it pays, but how exposed it is to scrutiny, penalties, and forced investigations, because the reality of today's regulatory environment is that audits are no longer random, slow, or limited by human capacity, but are now driven by artificial intelligence systems that scan millions of businesses in real time, comparing every transaction, deduction, payroll record, and financial pattern against vast databases of historical tax behavior to identify anomalies, inconsistencies, and risk signals, meaning that every business—whether it is a one-person online company, a real estate investor, a multi-state retailer, or a growing corporation—is continuously being scored by invisible machines that decide whether it deserves closer examination, and this new reality has fundamentally changed what it means to be "compliant," because being technically legal is no longer enough if your data patterns look suspicious to the algorithms that now power government enforcement, which is why this book exists, to show you how artificial intelligence can be used not only by tax authorities to detect risk but by your business to stay ahead of that risk, reduce audit probability, and create a digital shield around your finances that makes your company appear clean, organized, and low-risk in the eyes of every regulatory system that monitors it. For decades businesses have relied on reactive audit defense, hiring accountants and tax attorneys only after a letter arrives, scrambling to locate documents, reconstruct transactions, and justify decisions that were made months or years earlier, but in an AI-driven tax world that approach is dangerously outdated, because once an algorithm flags your business, the investigation process becomes fast, precise, and extremely difficult to stop, with every discrepancy instantly cross-checked against banking data, payment processors, payroll platforms, and third-party reporting systems, which means the real opportunity for protection happens long before an audit ever begins, through the intelligent design of your financial data, record-keeping, transaction flow, and reporting structure, all of which can now be guided and optimized by AI to make your business look exactly the way regulators want to see it: consistent, transparent, and statistically normal. This book introduces you to a new paradigm of audit defense—one that is proactive rather than reactive, automated rather than manual, and strategic rather than fearful—where artificial intelligence continuously monitors your financial activity, detects risk signals before they become problems, and helps you correct them while they are still invisible to the outside world, effectively turning compliance into an always-on system rather than a once-a-year event. In this new model your business no longer waits to be questioned; it is constantly aligning itself with the patterns that pass the scrutiny of the most advanced compliance algorithms on the planet, ensuring that what you file, what you report, and what you actually do all match in ways that reduce red flags and maximize credibility. The truth is that most audits are not triggered by wrongdoing but by inconsistency, because AI does not understand intent, ethics, or business reality, it understands numbers, patterns, and probabilities, and when your revenue, deductions, expenses, payroll, or asset usage fall outside expected ranges for your industry, size, or entity type, the system assigns risk, even if everything is technically legal, which means the smartest businesses are now using AI not just to prepare taxes but to shape the underlying financial story their data tells, ensuring that the story makes sense to machines before it ever reaches a human auditor. This is especially critical in an era of digital payments, where every transaction leaves a trail, and third-party reporting systems like payment processors, banks, payroll platforms, and e-commerce marketplaces automatically feed data into government systems, eliminating the privacy and flexibility that once allowed small businesses to operate under the radar, making consistency across all these data streams the new currency of safety. AI audit defense therefore begins with understanding how these systems see your business, how they compare you to millions of others, and how they decide what looks risky, and from there using technology to design your financial operations in ways that stay inside safe ranges without sacrificing profit, growth, or legal deductions. Throughout this book you will learn how AI models can analyze your historical filings, real-time transaction data, and industry benchmarks to calculate your audit risk score, identify weak points, and recommend adjustments that improve your compliance profile, whether that means changing how expenses are categorized, how income is recognized, how payroll is structured, or how asset depreciation is timed, all of which can be done automatically with modern accounting and tax-intelligence software that works continuously in the background. You will also see how artificial intelligence can create a digital audit trail that is far more powerful than traditional record keeping, because instead of scattered receipts and spreadsheets you will have structured, timestamped, and fully documented transaction histories that are instantly retrievable, making it easy to respond to any inquiry with precise, complete, and professionally organized data that satisfies even the most demanding investigators. This kind of AI-driven documentation does more than protect you during an audit; it often prevents one from happening at all, because regulators are far less likely to pursue businesses whose records appear clean, consistent, and low-risk, preferring instead to focus their limited resources on companies whose data looks chaotic, incomplete, or statistically abnormal. Another critical dimension of AI audit defense is predictive compliance, where machine learning models analyze changes in tax law, enforcement trends, and industry-specific audit behavior to forecast where future scrutiny will increase, allowing your business to adjust ahead of time, rather than reacting after penalties are assessed, which is especially valuable for growing companies, online businesses, and multi-entity structures that often operate in gray areas of tax code interpretation. With predictive AI you no longer have to guess whether a strategy is safe, because you can see how similar businesses have been treated, what patterns led to audits, and which structures consistently pass regulatory filters, giving you the ability to make decisions based on data rather than fear. This transforms tax compliance from a burden into a competitive advantage, because businesses that operate with AI-guided clarity can move faster, take more opportunities, and use more aggressive yet legal strategies, while those without it remain trapped in conservative, inefficient approaches driven by uncertainty and risk aversion. By the end of this book you will understand that audit defense is not about hiding, it is about being so clean, consistent, and well-documented that there is nothing worth investigating, and artificial intelligence is the tool that makes that possible at scale, across every transaction, every account, and every reporting obligation your business has. You will see how to integrate AI into your accounting systems, payment platforms, payroll tools, and tax software so that compliance becomes automated, risk becomes visible, and protection becomes continuous, creating a business that is not just profitable but resilient, not just compliant but strategically shielded, and not just reactive but intelligently designed to thrive in a world where machines, not people, are now the first line of tax enforcement. In the pages ahead this book will guide you through the mindset, technology, and operational framework needed to build an AI-powered audit defense system that protects your company from unnecessary scrutiny, costly penalties, and disruptive investigations, allowing you to focus on growth, innovation, and long-term wealth creation with confidence that your financial foundation is strong, transparent, and future-proof.

Chapter 1

The New Age of AI-Driven Audits

In the modern regulatory environment audits are no longer events that happen to a small unlucky fraction of businesses, they are a permanent background process driven by artificial intelligence systems that continuously analyze corporate financial behavior across millions of entities, meaning that every business is effectively under constant review whether it realizes it or not, because today's tax authorities do not wait for human examiners to randomly select cases but instead deploy massive machine learning platforms that compare each company's income, deductions, payroll, assets, banking activity, sales platforms, and vendor payments against enormous statistical models of what "normal" looks like for businesses of similar size, industry, and geography, and when a company's financial story deviates too far from those expected patterns it is quietly flagged for further scrutiny long before any letter is ever mailed, which makes understanding this invisible system the first step to surviving and thriving in a high-tech compliance world. These AI systems are fed by data from nearly every financial platform your business touches, including banks, credit card processors, payroll services, e-commerce platforms, real estate records, and payment apps, creating a complete digital shadow of your business that no longer depends on what you choose to report but instead on what the financial ecosystem already knows about you, and this means that the old strategy of "just file and hope" has been replaced by a new reality where mismatches between reported numbers and third-party data become automatic red flags that AI detects instantly, which is why even honest businesses get audited at increasing rates when their records are disorganized, inconsistent, or poorly structured. What makes this shift so powerful is that AI does not think in terms of guilt or innocence, it thinks in probabilities, assigning every business a risk score based on how likely it is that something is wrong, and when that score crosses a certain threshold the system escalates the case to human investigators who then look for evidence to justify what the algorithm already suspects, meaning that audit defense today is less about arguing after the fact and more about making sure your numbers never trigger those algorithms in the first place. This has led to the rise of algorithmic compliance, where businesses must not only follow the law but also appear statistically normal, because even legal deductions, aggressive depreciation, or unconventional income structures can look suspicious if they fall outside the patterns the AI has learned from millions of other companies, making it essential to understand not just tax rules but data patterns, because those patterns are what determine whether your business is left alone or pulled into a costly and stressful investigation. In this new environment artificial intelligence becomes both the threat and the solution, because while government systems use AI to detect anomalies, your business can use AI to simulate how its financial profile looks from the outside, identifying the same red flags before regulators ever see them and allowing you to adjust your bookkeeping, categorization, timing, and reporting in ways that lower risk without reducing profit. This is where AI-powered audit defense begins, with models that analyze your historical filings, real-time transactions, and industry benchmarks to create a digital mirror of how your company appears to enforcement systems, revealing whether your expense ratios are too high, your payroll too low, your depreciation too aggressive, or your income too volatile compared to similar businesses, and from there recommending precise changes that bring your profile back into safe ranges while preserving every legal advantage. This process is not about manipulation or hiding, it is about alignment, making sure that what you are doing and what the data shows are coherent, consistent, and credible, because credibility is the currency that AI-driven enforcement responds to. As these systems continue to evolve they are becoming better at detecting not just simple errors but complex strategies such as income shifting, entity arbitrage, and expense loading, which means that businesses that rely on outdated accounting methods or manual bookkeeping are operating blind in a world where machines see everything, while those that adopt AI-based compliance tools gain the ability to monitor themselves with the same sophistication as the regulators, turning compliance into an active management function rather than a passive annual chore. This also changes how audits themselves are conducted, because when an investigation begins it is no longer a slow back-and-forth of paper documents but a rapid data-driven process where auditors request digital records that are instantly cross-checked against external databases, meaning that businesses with disorganized or incomplete records quickly appear suspicious even if they did nothing wrong, while those with clean, well-structured, AI-generated audit trails can resolve inquiries quickly and often avoid deeper examination entirely. By integrating AI into your accounting, expense tracking, payroll, and tax preparation systems you create a living compliance layer that ensures every transaction is categorized correctly, every document is stored automatically, and every report matches across platforms, which dramatically reduces the chance that any algorithm will ever find something that looks off, giving your business a powerful invisible shield against unnecessary attention. As you move through this book you will learn how to build this shield, how to understand the risk signals that trigger audits, and how to use artificial intelligence to design a financial architecture that not only complies with the law but communicates trustworthiness to the machines that now enforce it, allowing your business to grow, invest, and innovate without living in fear of the next letter from the tax authorities.

"The Algorithm That Watched Everything"

Marcus Alvarez had built his digital logistics company from a laptop and a vision, scaling it from a one-man operation into a multi-million-dollar enterprise that processed thousands of transactions a day across multiple states and payment platforms, and from the outside everything looked perfect, with revenue growing steadily, customers happy, and expenses tightly managed, yet beneath the surface his financial world was fragmented across bank accounts, merchant processors, payroll systems, and accounting software that barely talked to each other, creating a messy digital footprint that no human could see all at once but that government algorithms could analyze in seconds, and Marcus never imagined that this invisible observer was quietly forming an opinion about his business until the day a certified letter arrived announcing an audit that threatened to derail everything he had built. At first he was confused because he knew he had done nothing illegal, he had paid his taxes, kept receipts, and followed the advice of his accountant, but what he did not understand was that his business had tripped an algorithmic wire, because his expense ratios were higher than average for his industry, his payroll was lower than expected for his revenue level, and his depreciation schedules were aggressive, all of which were perfectly legal but statistically unusual, causing the AI systems that monitored corporate filings to flag his company as high risk, sending it into a queue for human investigation. The auditors did not come with accusations, they came with data, showing Marcus charts and comparisons that made his business look strange, and suddenly he was forced to explain numbers he had never even thought about before, trying to justify why his digital model looked different from traditional companies, but the burden of proof was on him, and without a unified, AI-organized audit trail he struggled to provide clear answers quickly, which only made the auditors more suspicious. That was when he discovered the world of AI-driven compliance, learning that the same kind of machine learning that had flagged his business could also be used to protect it, by analyzing his entire financial ecosystem, finding inconsistencies, and restructuring how his data was presented to the outside world, and with the help of intelligent software he began to clean, categorize, and normalize his financial profile, creating a version of his business that not only told the truth but told it in a way that algorithms understood. As the weeks passed his AI system automatically reconciled transactions, corrected misclassifications, generated missing documentation, and produced reports that aligned perfectly across platforms, turning his chaotic digital footprint into a clear, coherent story that even the auditors could not question, and when he submitted this new data set the tone of the investigation shifted, because what had once looked risky now looked professional, organized, and low-threat, causing the regulators to lose interest and eventually close the case with no penalties. Marcus realized that he had not escaped because he was lucky but because he had learned how to speak the language of machines, understanding that in a world where algorithms watch everything, the safest businesses are not those that hide but those that are so well-documented and statistically aligned that there is nothing worth looking at, and from that moment on he made AI compliance a permanent part of his company, not just as a defense against audits but as a foundation for fearless growth, knowing that no matter how big his business became it would always be protected by an intelligent system that kept it clean, credible, and invisible to unnecessary scrutiny.

Chapter 2

How AI Calculates Your Audit Risk Score

Every business in the modern economy carries an invisible number that determines how likely it is to be investigated by tax authorities, and that number is not based on intuition, complaints, or chance but on algorithmic risk scoring systems that analyze your company's financial behavior in extraordinary detail, comparing it to millions of others in your industry, size range, and geographic footprint, and what makes this so powerful and so dangerous is that these systems do not look for fraud in the traditional sense but instead for statistical improbability, meaning they flag businesses whose income, expenses, payroll, deductions, asset usage, or growth patterns deviate too far from what their models expect to see, even if everything is technically legal, which is why understanding how AI builds and interprets your audit risk score is the single most important step in protecting your company from unwanted attention. These models are trained on decades of historical tax data, including past audits, penalties, adjustments, and enforcement outcomes, allowing them to learn what kinds of financial profiles are most often associated with errors, underreporting, aggressive deductions, or structural abuse, and once trained they continuously ingest fresh data from banks, payroll processors, merchant accounts, credit card networks, and filing systems, updating your risk score in near real time as your business operates, meaning that every transaction you make subtly shifts how the government's machines perceive you. A sudden spike in revenue without a corresponding increase in payroll, a large write-off in a year where profits are high, a pattern of round-number expenses, or an unusual mix of income sources can all push your risk score upward, because AI systems are designed to notice not just what you report but how you report it, detecting patterns that humans would never have the time or ability to analyze, which is why many businesses are shocked when they receive audit notices despite having done nothing intentionally wrong. The goal of AI audit defense is therefore not to reduce taxes by becoming more conservative but to reduce statistical risk by making sure that your financial profile looks coherent, consistent, and explainable to machines, which is where artificial intelligence becomes your greatest ally, because the same techniques used by regulators can be applied internally to simulate how your business is being evaluated, allowing you to see your own risk score, identify what is driving it, and make strategic adjustments before those signals ever reach enforcement systems. By feeding your financial data into AI compliance tools that mirror regulatory models you can see whether your expense ratios are too high for your revenue level, whether your depreciation schedules are out of sync with your asset base, whether your payroll is too low for your operational scale, or whether your income streams are too fragmented, and from there receive precise recommendations for how to rebalance those numbers through timing, categorization, or structural changes that preserve every legal benefit while bringing your profile back into safe statistical ranges. This process is incredibly powerful because it transforms compliance from a vague concept into a measurable, manageable variable, turning audit risk into something you can track, optimize, and control just like cash flow or profit margin, and when you do this consistently your business begins to operate inside an invisible corridor of safety where every filing, payment, and deduction reinforces a low-risk pattern that keeps regulators' algorithms satisfied. AI also makes it possible to run predictive simulations, allowing you to test how future decisions—such as purchasing new equipment, hiring contractors, changing entity structures, or expanding into new states—will affect your risk score before you commit to them, giving you the ability to choose strategies that maximize profit while minimizing audit exposure, which is especially important for fast-growing or highly leveraged businesses where one misaligned move can suddenly make their data look abnormal. Over time this creates a powerful feedback loop in which your AI systems continuously analyze new transactions, update your risk profile, and suggest small adjustments that keep everything aligned, ensuring that your business never drifts into the kind of statistical territory that attracts attention, and this is what separates companies that live in fear of audits from those that operate with confidence, knowing that their financial data is constantly being shaped and optimized for both profitability and protection. In this chapter you will learn how to interpret the key variables that drive audit risk, how AI models weigh different financial signals, and how to build your own internal risk dashboard that shows you exactly where your business stands at any given moment, giving you the power to turn what was once an unpredictable threat into a controllable part of your overall financial strategy.

"The Score That Decided Everything"

Sophia Grant had spent years building her e-commerce empire, selling specialty wellness products through multiple online marketplaces, and from the outside her business looked like a textbook success story, with revenue growing every quarter and customers pouring in from across the country, yet behind the scenes she had never considered how her numbers looked to the algorithms that monitored every transaction, because to her they were just numbers in a dashboard, not signals being judged by invisible machines, and it was only when her tax advisor casually mentioned that her audit risk seemed unusually high that she realized something was wrong. Confused and alarmed, Sophia began using an AI compliance platform that analyzed her entire financial footprint, pulling data from her payment processors, advertising accounts, inventory systems, and payroll records, and within minutes it produced a risk score that was far higher than she expected, not because she had cheated but because her expense ratios, contractor payments, and rapid revenue growth created a pattern that the models associated with aggressive or error-prone businesses, making her a prime candidate for future scrutiny. At first she felt angry, because she had followed the rules, but as she studied the AI's breakdown she began to understand that the system was not judging her intentions but her statistical profile, and that profile looked unusual compared to thousands of similar companies, which meant she was being quietly watched whether she liked it or not. Instead of panicking she decided to take control, using the AI's recommendations to adjust how she categorized advertising costs, how she timed inventory purchases, and how she structured payments to contractors, making small changes that brought her ratios back into alignment with industry norms without sacrificing growth, and as weeks passed her risk score began to drop, reflecting a financial story that now looked cleaner, more consistent, and less alarming to the algorithms that evaluated her. Months later when a wave of audits swept through her industry Sophia's business was untouched, while several competitors were pulled into costly investigations, and she realized that the difference was not luck but data, because she had learned to see her business the way machines saw it and to shape that perception using AI, turning what had once been an invisible threat into a measurable, manageable shield that allowed her to keep growing with confidence, knowing that behind every sale, every expense, and every report there was an intelligent system quietly keeping her safe.

Chapter 3

Building an AI-Powered Digital Audit Trail

In an era where every transaction leaves a digital footprint and every financial platform shares data with regulatory systems, the most powerful form of audit protection is not secrecy but precision, because what regulators and their algorithms are really looking for is not proof of wrongdoing but the absence of clarity, and when records are incomplete, inconsistent, or difficult to verify they become magnets for deeper investigation, which is why the concept of an AI-powered digital audit trail has become the foundation of modern compliance, transforming scattered receipts, spreadsheets, and bank statements into a unified, intelligent record that can explain every dollar your business touches in a way that both humans and machines can instantly understand. A digital audit trail is far more than a folder of documents; it is a continuously updated system of linked data that connects each transaction to its source, purpose, category, and supporting evidence, and when artificial intelligence is applied to this system it becomes self-organizing, self-validating, and self-correcting, automatically pulling information from banks, payment processors, payroll platforms, invoicing tools, and accounting software to create a living map of your company's financial reality that no human bookkeeper could ever assemble manually. What makes this so powerful in the context of audit defense is that AI does not just store data, it understands relationships, recognizing how a vendor payment connects to a project, how a payroll expense ties to revenue, and how a depreciation entry aligns with an asset purchase, allowing it to detect missing links, misclassifications, or inconsistencies in real time and fix them before they become red flags for regulators. This means that instead of scrambling to reconstruct months or years of financial activity when an audit notice arrives, businesses with AI-powered audit trails can instantly produce complete, structured, and verifiable records that show exactly what happened, why it happened, and how it was reported, making audits faster, less stressful, and far less likely to escalate. Another critical advantage of AI-driven audit trails is their ability to standardize how data is recorded and presented across all systems, because one of the biggest triggers for audits is mismatched information between tax filings, bank records, and third-party reports, and AI solves this by continuously reconciling these data streams, flagging discrepancies, and correcting them at the source, ensuring that what you report always matches what the financial ecosystem already knows about your business. This level of consistency is incredibly valuable in a world where enforcement algorithms are trained to look for contradictions, because when every platform tells the same story your risk score drops, your credibility rises, and your business becomes statistically uninteresting to regulators who are programmed to chase anomalies rather than well-documented companies. AI also enables the creation of predictive audit trails, where future transactions are modeled before they happen, allowing businesses to see how a large purchase, a change in payroll, or a new revenue stream will affect their documentation and risk profile, giving them the ability to structure deals in ways that keep records clean and compliant from the start rather than fixing problems later. Over time this creates a powerful cycle of trust between your business and the regulatory systems that monitor it, because every year your filings become easier to verify, every inquiry becomes simpler to answer, and every audit becomes less intrusive, which not only saves money on accountants and legal fees but also protects your company's reputation, creditworthiness, and operational focus. By building an AI-powered digital audit trail you are not just preparing for audits, you are redesigning your financial infrastructure to speak the language of machines, ensuring that no matter how complex your business becomes, its financial story remains clear, consistent, and defensible, giving you the freedom to grow, invest, and innovate without the constant fear that one missing receipt or misclassified expense will suddenly put everything at risk.

"The File That Never Lost a Page"

When Daniel Mercer launched his commercial real estate holding company he believed that success was measured by how many properties he could acquire and how fast he could scale, and for years that approach worked, as buildings, tenants, and cash flow piled up, but behind the scenes his financial records became a maze of spreadsheets, email receipts, property management reports, and bank statements that no one fully understood, not even his accountants, creating a fragile system that only seemed stable because no one had yet pulled too hard on any single thread. That illusion shattered when a routine inquiry from a tax authority turned into a full audit, with requests for years of transaction histories, depreciation schedules, and expense justifications arriving faster than his team could respond, and for the first time Daniel realized that it was not the numbers themselves that were hurting him but the lack of a clear, unified story behind them. Desperate for a solution he turned to an AI-powered compliance platform that promised to build a digital audit trail for his entire company, and within weeks the system had ingested data from every account, every property, and every vendor, automatically linking payments to leases, repairs to work orders, and depreciation to asset purchases, creating a living financial map that finally made sense of the chaos. As the AI continued to learn it began filling in gaps, finding missing invoices, correcting misclassified expenses, and reconciling discrepancies between reports, until what had once been a tangled mess became a clean, coherent record that could answer any question in seconds. When Daniel submitted this new audit package to the investigators their tone changed almost immediately, because instead of seeing confusion they saw clarity, and instead of hunting for errors they found a company whose financial story was complete, transparent, and easy to verify, leading them to close the case with minimal adjustments. Walking away from the experience Daniel realized that the real asset he had built was not just a portfolio of properties but a system that made his business understandable to machines, and in a world where algorithms decide who gets scrutinized, that clarity was the most powerful form of protection he could ever own.

Chapter 4

Real-Time AI Monitoring, Alerts, and Preemptive Risk Correction

In the age of artificial intelligence, the most effective audit defense is no longer something that happens annually at tax time but something that operates continuously in the background of a business, quietly watching every transaction, every classification, and every reporting decision as it happens, because the true danger in modern compliance is not a single mistake but the accumulation of small inconsistencies that gradually elevate a company's risk profile until it crosses an invisible threshold and attracts regulatory attention, which is why real-time AI monitoring has become the final and most powerful layer of audit protection, transforming compliance from a retrospective exercise into a proactive, living system. Unlike traditional accounting processes that look backward and attempt to clean up problems after the fact, AI-driven monitoring systems analyze financial activity as it occurs, evaluating each new transaction against historical data, industry benchmarks, and regulatory patterns to determine whether it strengthens or weakens the company's overall compliance posture, allowing risks to be identified and corrected while they are still microscopic and before they ever appear in official filings. This real-time capability fundamentally changes how businesses interact with risk, because instead of discovering problems months later during reconciliation or audits, companies receive immediate alerts when something looks off, such as an expense category drifting out of normal range, a payroll ratio falling below expected thresholds, revenue spikes that are not matched by operational indicators, or documentation gaps that could later be interpreted as negligence. These alerts are not generic warnings but context-aware insights generated by machine learning models that understand the unique structure, growth stage, and industry characteristics of each business, meaning they can distinguish between healthy anomalies caused by growth and dangerous anomalies that are statistically associated with audits, penalties, or investigations. Once a risk is detected, AI systems can do more than simply notify humans; they can recommend or even automatically implement corrective actions, such as reclassifying expenses, adjusting accrual timing, requesting missing documentation from vendors, reconciling mismatched records across platforms, or flagging transactions for review before they are finalized, effectively creating a self-healing financial system that continuously steers the business back toward compliance without interrupting operations. This preemptive correction capability is especially powerful because most audits are triggered not by deliberate misconduct but by unresolved inconsistencies that compound over time, and AI prevents this compounding effect by ensuring that every small issue is addressed immediately, keeping the overall data profile clean and stable. Another critical advantage of real-time AI monitoring is its ability to adapt as laws, enforcement priorities, and regulatory technologies evolve, because machine learning systems can be retrained on new data, updated enforcement trends, and emerging audit patterns, allowing them to adjust risk thresholds and alert logic dynamically, ensuring that businesses remain protected even as the rules of the game change. This adaptability is essential in a world where tax authorities increasingly experiment with new analytical techniques, data sources, and compliance programs, because a static compliance strategy quickly becomes obsolete, while an AI-driven one evolves alongside the systems it is designed to satisfy. Over time businesses that implement real-time AI monitoring develop an entirely different relationship with compliance, viewing it not as a burden or a source of anxiety but as an automated safeguard that quietly supports growth, innovation, and decision-making by ensuring that every move is made within a statistically safe and defensible framework. By the end of this chapter you will understand how to design and deploy real-time AI monitoring systems that watch your business with the same sophistication as regulatory algorithms, how to interpret and act on AI-generated alerts, and how to build workflows that correct risk automatically, creating a company that is not only compliant on paper but continuously aligned with the invisible expectations of the machines that now govern audit selection, allowing you to operate with confidence, speed, and peace of mind in an increasingly automated regulatory world.

"The Business That Never Slept"

Ethan Cole used to believe that control meant oversight, that as long as he reviewed reports, trusted his accountants, and checked in on his numbers once a month, his fast-growing SaaS company was safe, but what he did not realize was that while his team slept, while his dashboards refreshed, and while his spreadsheets closed for the day, an entirely different set of systems never stopped watching, silently evaluating every subscription payment, refund, payroll run, and vendor invoice against massive models of expected behavior, and by the time Ethan noticed something was wrong it would already be too late. His company had grown rapidly, expanding internationally, onboarding contractors across borders, experimenting with pricing, and reinvesting aggressively, and while the growth felt exciting, the underlying financial data became increasingly complex, with timing differences, currency conversions, and platform integrations creating subtle inconsistencies that no single human could fully track in real time, even though those inconsistencies were accumulating into patterns that looked unusual to the machines monitoring him. The first sign of trouble was not a letter but a quiet warning from an AI compliance platform his CFO insisted they test, a system that scanned their live data and produced a dashboard showing elevated risk signals that none of them expected, highlighting mismatches between revenue growth and payroll scaling, unusual expense timing caused by international vendors, and documentation gaps created by rapid onboarding, all of which were legal and explainable but statistically abnormal, pushing the company's invisible risk score steadily upward. At first Ethan dismissed the warnings as overly cautious, but as the AI continued monitoring it began issuing increasingly specific alerts, showing how if the current trajectory continued the company would cross a risk threshold within months, not because of wrongdoing but because the data story was becoming harder to reconcile, and that realization shook him, because he understood that regulators would not see intention, innovation, or growth, they would only see numbers that didn't line up neatly with expectations. Reluctantly he agreed to let the system intervene, and what followed felt almost surreal, as the AI began working continuously, flagging transactions before they were finalized, requesting missing contracts automatically, reconciling discrepancies between platforms overnight, and suggesting small adjustments to timing and categorization that gradually brought the company's profile back into alignment, all without slowing the business down or requiring constant meetings. Weeks turned into months, and as the company continued to grow faster than ever, something strange happened: the risk alerts diminished, the dashboards stabilized, and the AI showed a steadily declining audit probability, even as revenue doubled, because the system was quietly shaping the data into a coherent, defensible narrative in real time. One afternoon news broke that several competitors in Ethan's space had been hit with audits related to international contractor classification and revenue recognition, causing panic across the industry, yet Ethan's company received nothing, no letters, no inquiries, no disruption, and it was in that moment that he finally understood the value of a business that never slept, one protected by an intelligent system that watched continuously, corrected silently, and ensured that while the world's algorithms were always observing, there was never anything alarming enough to stop and look twice.

Chapter 5

AI-Guided Audit Response, Defense Strategy, and Resolution

Even with the most advanced preventive systems in place, there are moments when a business must respond directly to regulatory inquiries, and in an AI-driven enforcement environment the difference between a brief review and a prolonged, costly audit often comes down to how intelligently and strategically that response is executed, because modern audits are no longer exploratory fishing expeditions but targeted data-verification exercises guided by algorithms that already suspect where inconsistencies may exist, making it critical that every interaction, document submission, and explanation reinforces credibility rather than uncertainty. Artificial intelligence transforms audit response from a reactive scramble into a structured, data-backed process by organizing information exactly the way regulators expect to see it, anticipating follow-up questions, and ensuring that every answer aligns perfectly with previously reported data, third-party records, and industry benchmarks. Instead of relying on memory, guesswork, or manual document searches, AI-powered audit response systems instantly assemble comprehensive audit packets that include transaction histories, supporting documentation, reconciliations, and contextual explanations, all formatted in a way that reduces friction for investigators and minimizes opportunities for misinterpretation. This is crucial because auditors are trained, and increasingly assisted by their own AI tools, to escalate cases when responses are slow, incomplete, or confusing, whereas clear, immediate, and well-organized submissions often signal that deeper investigation will yield little value, encouraging faster resolution. AI also plays a key role in shaping audit defense strategy by analyzing the scope of the inquiry, identifying which areas carry the highest risk, and recommending how to frame responses in ways that stay factual, consistent, and narrow, avoiding unnecessary disclosures that could expand the audit beyond its original focus. This strategic containment is one of the most overlooked aspects of audit defense, because many businesses inadvertently invite deeper scrutiny by oversharing, speculating, or providing unstructured data that raises new questions, whereas AI-guided responses are designed to answer exactly what is asked, no more and no less, maintaining control over the narrative. During an active audit AI systems can continuously monitor new requests, cross-check proposed responses against historical filings, and flag potential contradictions before they are submitted, acting as a final safeguard that ensures nothing undermines the company's credibility. Over time this capability becomes even more powerful, because AI learns from past audits, resolutions, and enforcement outcomes, refining its recommendations based on what has proven effective, allowing businesses to develop an institutional memory that grows stronger with each interaction rather than repeating the same costly mistakes. When used correctly AI does not replace human advisors but amplifies them, giving accountants and attorneys a clearer picture, faster access to information, and data-driven insights that improve decision-making under pressure. By the end of this chapter you will understand how to deploy AI during every phase of an audit, from the first notice to final resolution, how to maintain narrative control, how to reduce escalation risk, and how to emerge from scrutiny with your business not only intact but stronger, more credible, and better prepared for the future.

"The Day the Questions Arrived"

When the letter finally arrived, it did not feel dramatic, it did not threaten, and it did not accuse, which somehow made it more terrifying to Olivia Bennett than anything else could have, because it was calm, precise, and methodical, requesting specific records related to revenue recognition, contractor payments, and expense categorization over a defined period, signaling that whoever—or whatever—had initiated the inquiry already knew where to look, and that realization made Olivia understand instantly that this was not a random audit but the result of something far more calculated. Olivia had built her consulting firm carefully over a decade, scaling it from solo practice to a multi-entity operation serving clients across industries and borders, and while she prided herself on integrity and transparency, she also knew that growth had brought complexity, complexity had brought fragmentation, and fragmentation had created a data trail that might not tell the clean story she believed it did. Her first instinct was panic, a familiar human response, as she imagined endless document requests, months of disruption, and the possibility that something small and overlooked could spiral into something catastrophic, but before she could react emotionally her operations director reminded her that two years earlier they had implemented an AI compliance and audit response platform precisely for this moment, and suddenly the fear was replaced by cautious focus. As the system ingested the audit notice it immediately mapped the scope, identifying which entities, accounts, and periods were implicated, then began assembling a structured response package, pulling transaction data, contracts, invoices, and reconciliations into a unified framework that mirrored regulatory expectations, while also flagging areas where explanations might be required due to statistical deviations that were legal but potentially confusing.

Watching the system work felt surreal to Olivia, as if a second brain had come online, calmly analyzing, organizing, and anticipating in ways that no human team could replicate under pressure, and when the first draft response was ready it was not a pile of documents but a clear, coherent narrative supported by evidence, explaining not just what the numbers were but why they made sense in the context of her business model. As follow-up questions arrived, each more specific than the last, the AI adapted in real time, narrowing responses, cross-checking consistency, and warning Olivia's advisors when a proposed answer might inadvertently expand the audit's scope, helping them stay disciplined and precise even as stress levels rose. Weeks passed, then months, yet unlike the horror stories Olivia had heard from peers, the audit never seemed to spiral, because every request was met quickly, clearly, and confidently, leaving little room for doubt or suspicion, and eventually the tone of the correspondence changed, becoming procedural rather than probing, until one final notice arrived stating that the review was complete with no material findings. When Olivia read those words she felt an overwhelming sense of relief, but also a profound shift in perspective, realizing that the true power of AI had not been in preventing the audit or magically eliminating risk, but in transforming a moment of potential chaos into a controlled, navigable process that preserved her business, her reputation, and her peace of mind. Long after the audit closed she kept the system running, not out of fear but out of respect for a world where questions are inevitable, machines are always watching, and the businesses that survive are not the ones that hope for the best, but the ones that are always ready to answer with clarity, confidence, and control.

Chapter 6

Long-Term Audit Immunity Through AI-Driven Compliance Architecture

True audit protection is not achieved by surviving a single investigation but by building a business so structurally aligned with regulatory expectations that audits become increasingly unlikely over time, and in an AI-governed enforcement world this level of immunity can only be achieved by designing compliance into the very architecture of how a company operates, because when artificial intelligence systems evaluate businesses year after year they are not just looking at isolated filings but at longitudinal behavior, tracking consistency, improvement, responsiveness, and credibility across time, which means that businesses that demonstrate stable, explainable patterns gradually move into a low-priority category while those that fluctuate, experiment chaotically, or fail to evolve become persistent targets for scrutiny. AI-driven compliance architecture is the discipline of intentionally structuring systems, workflows, and decision-making processes so that every financial action reinforces a coherent and defensible narrative over the long term, creating what can best be described as audit immunity, not because audits are impossible, but because there is little incentive for regulators to invest resources in businesses whose data history consistently confirms low risk. This architecture begins with integration, ensuring that accounting platforms, banking systems, payroll tools, invoicing software, tax preparation systems, and compliance dashboards all operate from a single source of truth, continuously reconciled and validated by AI models that eliminate discrepancies before they harden into historical records. From there AI introduces standardization, applying consistent categorization rules, documentation requirements, and reporting formats across years, entities, and jurisdictions, which is critical because enforcement algorithms reward stability and penalize variance, even when variance is legal, meaning that businesses that constantly change how they report, classify, or structure transactions appear unpredictable and therefore riskier. Another essential component of long-term compliance architecture is institutional memory, where AI systems retain contextual understanding of past decisions, audits, explanations, and resolutions, allowing future filings to remain consistent with historical narratives rather than inadvertently contradicting them, which is a common trigger for renewed scrutiny when businesses grow or restructure. AI also enables progressive optimization, where each tax year becomes cleaner, more aligned, and more defensible than the last, because machine learning models analyze prior outcomes, adjust thresholds, and refine workflows to reduce risk incrementally, creating a compounding effect that steadily lowers audit probability while maintaining or even improving profitability. This long-term perspective fundamentally changes how businesses approach tax planning, moving away from short-term tactics that maximize deductions in isolation and toward holistic strategies that balance savings, risk, and narrative coherence across multiple years, entities, and regulatory regimes. By embedding AI into governance structures, approval workflows, and strategic planning processes, businesses ensure that every major decision—whether it involves expansion, restructuring, asset acquisition, or revenue diversification—is evaluated not only for financial impact but for its effect on long-term compliance posture, preventing sudden shifts that could trigger algorithmic attention. Over time this creates a business that regulators come to recognize as predictable, transparent, and self-correcting, characteristics that AI-driven enforcement systems implicitly trust, reducing the likelihood of audits, shortening the duration of reviews, and minimizing the severity of outcomes when inquiries do occur. By the end of this chapter you will understand how to design and maintain an AI-driven compliance architecture that evolves with your business, strengthens with each tax year, and quietly builds a reputation of low risk and high credibility in the eyes of the machines that now decide who gets examined and who is left alone.

"The Company the System Learned to Trust"

For most of his career Jonathan Reeves believed that success meant growth, and growth meant risk, and that audits were simply the price ambitious businesses paid for moving faster than the rest, a belief reinforced every time a colleague complained about regulatory scrutiny or another industry headline warned of increased enforcement, so when he founded his advanced manufacturing firm he accepted audits as inevitable, something to endure rather than avoid, until a mentor asked him a single question that quietly unsettled everything he thought he knew: "What if the system isn't punishing growth, but inconsistency?" At first Jonathan dismissed the idea, but as his company expanded across states, added automation, and integrated complex supply chains, he began to notice a pattern, watching competitors of similar size and revenue face repeated audits while his own business remained largely untouched, not because he was more conservative, but because years earlier he had invested in an AI-driven compliance framework that quietly shaped every financial decision the company made, and while he had initially adopted it to reduce operational friction, he was now realizing that it had been building something far more valuable in the background. The system had learned his company's rhythms, its seasonal fluctuations, its capital cycles, and its labor structure, and over time it had guided reporting decisions, flagged potential inconsistencies, and preserved a stable narrative that evolved smoothly rather than abruptly, making the company's financial history look less like a series of disconnected events and more like a coherent story unfolding predictably year after year. When Jonathan looked back over a decade of filings he saw a progression that felt almost intentional, with each year reinforcing the last, even as revenue tripled, facilities expanded, and markets shifted, and he realized that the AI had not just been reacting to risk but actively shaping the company's behavior to remain legible and trustworthy to the enforcement systems watching it. The true test came during an industry-wide compliance sweep triggered by new regulations, when dozens of firms received notices and scrambled to respond, while Jonathan's company received a brief inquiry that closed almost as soon as it opened, the regulators apparently satisfied by a data history that aligned so perfectly with expectations that further investigation offered little value. Sitting in his office after the news broke Jonathan finally understood what audit immunity really meant, not invincibility, but irrelevance, the quiet power of being so consistently compliant, so predictably structured, and so transparently documented that the machines tasked with finding problems simply moved on, and from that moment on he stopped thinking of AI compliance as a defensive expense and began seeing it as a foundational asset, one that allowed his company to grow boldly without fear, knowing that year after year the system was learning to trust him, and that trust was the rarest and most valuable currency in a world run by algorithms.

Chapter 7

From Audit Anxiety to Strategic Advantage: Turning Compliance Into Power

For most business owners the idea of an audit triggers anxiety, defensiveness, and a deep sense of vulnerability, because audits have historically represented moments when control is lost and decisions are questioned under pressure, yet in an AI-driven regulatory environment this mindset is not only outdated but counterproductive, because the same systems that create audit risk can also be harnessed to convert compliance into a strategic advantage that strengthens decision-making, improves financial clarity, and supports sustainable growth. When artificial intelligence is integrated deeply into compliance workflows it stops being a reactive shield and becomes a forward-looking compass, guiding businesses toward structures, behaviors, and reporting patterns that are not merely acceptable to regulators but actively favored by enforcement algorithms trained to reward consistency, transparency, and responsiveness. This shift fundamentally changes the role compliance plays inside an organization, transforming it from a cost center into an intelligence layer that informs strategy, reveals inefficiencies, and highlights opportunities for optimization that would otherwise remain hidden beneath surface-level financial statements. AI-powered compliance systems analyze not just what happened but why it happened and how it compares to both historical behavior and industry-wide patterns, allowing leadership teams to see their business the way regulators see it while simultaneously gaining insights that improve operational performance, capital allocation, and risk management. Over time businesses that embrace this approach begin to notice a compounding effect, where each clean filing, each well-documented decision, and each resolved inquiry strengthens their credibility profile, reducing future scrutiny while increasing confidence among lenders, partners, and investors who increasingly rely on data-driven assessments of risk. This credibility becomes a strategic asset, enabling faster approvals, better financing terms, smoother expansions, and greater flexibility in tax planning, because organizations that demonstrate disciplined, AI-guided compliance are perceived as lower risk across the entire financial ecosystem. Importantly this does not require becoming conservative or avoiding complexity, but rather managing complexity intelligently, using AI to ensure that even aggressive growth strategies are executed within a coherent, explainable framework that maintains alignment across years and entities. In this way compliance evolves from something businesses endure into something they leverage, a source of strength rather than fear, because when every decision is informed by real-time risk awareness and long-term narrative consistency, audits lose their power to disrupt, intimidate, or derail momentum. By the end of this chapter you will understand how to reframe compliance as a strategic discipline, how to use AI insights to support smarter growth decisions, and how to build a culture where audit readiness is not a reaction to threat but a natural outcome of intelligent, well-designed business operations that thrive under scrutiny rather than shrinking from it.

"When the Numbers Started Working for Them"

At the beginning of her career Rachel Kim believed that compliance was something you tolerated on the way to success, a necessary inconvenience that came bundled with entrepreneurship, and like many founders she focused her energy on clients, revenue, and innovation while leaving taxes, reporting, and documentation to advisors she trusted to handle it quietly in the background, never imagining that those unseen systems would one day become central to her company's fate. Her digital marketing firm grew quickly, expanding into new verticals, acquiring smaller agencies, and experimenting with performance-based compensation models that rewarded results rather than hours, and while the business flourished creatively, its financial footprint became increasingly complex, with revenue streams that did not fit neatly into traditional categories and cost structures that fluctuated wildly based on campaign performance. For years this complexity went largely unnoticed, until subtle signals began appearing in the form of delayed filings, follow-up questions from banks, and unusually detailed information requests that hinted something deeper was happening, though no one could quite explain what it was. It was only after a trusted advisor suggested implementing an AI-driven compliance intelligence system that Rachel began to see her business through a different lens, watching as the platform mapped her financial data, analyzed patterns across years, and produced a risk profile that told a story she had never considered, showing how her company's creativity and flexibility translated into statistical volatility that algorithms associated with uncertainty, even though every dollar was legitimate. At first the realization was unsettling, because it meant that success itself had created risk, but as Rachel dug deeper she began to see opportunity where she had once seen threat, recognizing that if AI could identify weaknesses it could also guide improvements that made the business stronger, not smaller. Slowly the company began making adjustments, not by changing its vision but by structuring its execution more intentionally, smoothing reporting transitions, standardizing documentation, and using AI insights to time strategic moves in ways that preserved momentum while maintaining narrative consistency, and over time the dashboards reflected a quiet transformation, with risk indicators declining even as revenue continued to climb. What surprised Rachel most was how these changes began influencing decisions far beyond compliance, shaping hiring plans, pricing strategies, and expansion timelines in ways that felt more grounded and deliberate, because the AI was not telling her what she could not do but showing her how to do it in ways that aligned with long-term credibility. The true turning point came when her firm pursued a major partnership with a global brand that conducted exhaustive due diligence using automated risk assessment tools, a process that would have been nerve-wracking in the past but now unfolded smoothly, as the company's clean, consistent data profile passed every check without issue, leading to an agreement that doubled the firm's scale almost overnight. Sitting in the aftermath of the deal Rachel reflected on how dramatically her relationship with compliance had changed, realizing that what she once feared had become a source of leverage, a silent ally that strengthened every negotiation, every expansion, and every strategic choice. Years later when peers asked her how she slept at night running such a complex operation in an increasingly regulated world, she would smile and explain that she no longer worried about audits or scrutiny, not because they could never happen, but because her business had learned how to thrive in the light, using intelligence, structure, and consistency to turn the very systems designed to find problems into proof that it was built to last.

Chapter 8

AI, Human Judgment, and the Future of Defensible Decision-Making

As artificial intelligence becomes the primary mechanism through which audits are initiated, evaluated, and resolved, the most resilient businesses are those that understand a crucial truth: long-term audit safety does not come from surrendering judgment to machines, nor from resisting them, but from creating a disciplined partnership between AI intelligence and human intent, because while algorithms excel at detecting patterns, anomalies, and probabilities, they lack the contextual understanding, ethical reasoning, and strategic foresight that define sound business judgment. In an AI-driven enforcement environment defensible decision-making becomes the ultimate form of protection, meaning that every significant financial choice must not only be legal and profitable but also explainable, consistent, and justifiable across time, entities, and scenarios, a standard that cannot be achieved through automation alone. AI provides the analytical foundation for this standard by modeling regulatory expectations, tracking risk signals, and highlighting potential consequences before decisions are finalized, but it is human leadership that must interpret those insights, weigh trade-offs, and decide how to act in ways that align with both business objectives and long-term credibility. This collaboration transforms decision-making from a series of isolated tactical moves into a cohesive strategic process, where every action reinforces a broader narrative of intentionality and responsibility that regulators' algorithms implicitly trust. One of the most powerful ways AI supports defensible decision-making is by documenting rationale, capturing not just what was done but why it was done, creating a living record of intent that can be referenced years later during audits, reviews, or disputes, which is increasingly important as enforcement systems evolve to evaluate not only outcomes but decision consistency over time. When AI systems are integrated into approval workflows, governance structures, and strategic planning, they act as guardians of coherence, ensuring that similar decisions are handled similarly, that exceptions are justified and documented, and that changes in strategy are implemented gradually and transparently rather than abruptly, reducing the appearance of volatility that triggers algorithmic suspicion. This approach also empowers leadership teams to make bolder, smarter moves, because instead of guessing how regulators might react, they can simulate outcomes, assess risk trajectories, and choose paths that maximize upside while preserving defensibility, turning AI from a constraint into a confidence-building tool. As enforcement technology becomes more sophisticated, businesses that rely solely on compliance checklists or manual oversight will struggle to keep pace, while those that cultivate this AI-human partnership will gain a durable advantage, operating with clarity in an environment where uncertainty is increasingly penalized. By the end of this chapter you will understand how to design decision frameworks that integrate AI insights without sacrificing human judgment, how to document intent in ways that strengthen audit defense, and how to future-proof your organization by making defensible decision-making a core capability rather than an afterthought.

"The Decision They Could Explain Years Later"

When Elena Morales approved the acquisition, she knew it would change everything, not just for her company but for her own sense of responsibility as its leader, because the deal was ambitious, unconventional, and likely to draw attention in an environment where algorithms watched every move, yet it also felt necessary, the kind of strategic leap that defined whether a business plateaued or evolved. Elena had built her data analytics firm carefully over fifteen years, growing it through steady contracts, disciplined hiring, and a culture that valued clarity over speed, but the market was shifting, competitors were consolidating, and clients were demanding broader capabilities, pushing her toward a decision that could not be made lightly. Before signing anything she turned to the AI governance platform her company had adopted years earlier, not because she expected it to decide for her, but because she wanted to understand how the acquisition would look through the eyes of systems that did not care about vision or ambition, only patterns, probabilities, and precedent. The simulations were sobering, showing how a sudden jump in revenue, debt, and asset complexity could elevate the company's risk profile if handled poorly, yet they also revealed pathways where the same move, structured differently and phased deliberately, could be absorbed smoothly, maintaining statistical coherence while unlocking growth. Over weeks of analysis, discussion, and refinement Elena and her leadership team used the AI not as an oracle but as a mirror, testing assumptions, documenting rationale, and aligning each step of the plan with a narrative that made sense both operationally and regulatorily, capturing decisions, alternatives considered, and reasons chosen in a system that would remember long after memories faded. When the acquisition closed it unfolded exactly as modeled, with integration milestones paced intentionally, reporting structures adjusted proactively, and documentation generated automatically, creating a trail of intent that made every choice legible and defensible. Years later, when a regulatory review examined the period surrounding the acquisition, what could have become a disruptive investigation turned into a routine verification, because every question had an answer, every change had a documented reason, and every outcome aligned with expectations set years earlier, leaving little room for doubt or suspicion. Sitting in her office after the review concluded Elena reflected on how different the experience felt compared to stories she had heard from peers, realizing that the true value of AI had not been in predicting risk or avoiding scrutiny, but in helping her become a better decision-maker, one who could act boldly while remaining accountable, confident that no matter how much time passed, her choices would still make sense to anyone, human or machine, who came looking.

Chapter 9

Surviving and Thriving After an Audit: AI as a Post-Audit Intelligence Engine

For many businesses an audit feels like an ending, a stressful interruption that finally concludes with relief or exhaustion, but in an AI-driven regulatory world the true impact of an audit is not confined to its resolution, because once a business has been examined it becomes part of a long-term data history that enforcement algorithms continue to evaluate, meaning that how a company evolves after scrutiny is often more important than how it performed before it. Artificial intelligence transforms the post-audit period from a passive recovery phase into an active intelligence cycle, where every outcome, adjustment, and interaction becomes valuable data that can be used to strengthen future compliance, reduce long-term risk, and improve strategic clarity. When an audit closes—whether with no findings, minor adjustments, or significant changes—AI systems can analyze the entire lifecycle of the investigation, identifying what triggered it, which responses were most effective, where friction occurred, and how enforcement behavior aligned with or deviated from expectations, turning what would otherwise be institutional amnesia into a permanent learning asset. This is critical because regulatory systems themselves learn, adapting their models based on audit outcomes, and businesses that fail to learn alongside them risk repeating patterns that quietly elevate risk over time. By capturing post-audit insights, AI enables companies to recalibrate their compliance architecture, adjust thresholds, refine documentation practices, and realign decision frameworks so that the conditions that led to scrutiny are systematically reduced rather than merely avoided temporarily. This process also helps organizations recover psychologically and operationally, replacing fear-driven conservatism with data-backed confidence, because leadership teams can see clearly which behaviors were truly problematic and which were benign but misunderstood, allowing them to move forward intelligently rather than retreating unnecessarily. AI-driven post-audit analysis also strengthens narrative continuity, ensuring that future filings, explanations, and decisions remain consistent with positions taken during the audit, which is essential because contradictions across time are a major trigger for renewed scrutiny, even when each action in isolation is legal. Over the long term businesses that treat audits as intelligence events rather than punishments develop a durable advantage, because each encounter with regulators makes them more refined, more coherent, and more predictable in ways that enforcement algorithms implicitly trust. In this way AI closes the compliance loop, transforming audits from disruptive threats into inflection points that strengthen resilience, improve governance, and reinforce credibility, ensuring that each year the business becomes less interesting to regulators and more confident in its ability to operate under observation.

"After the Silence"

When the audit finally ended, the silence felt almost unnatural to Michael Harper, as if the constant hum of anticipation, document requests, and careful wording had been replaced by a vacuum that his mind did not know how to fill, because for nearly a year his company's existence had revolved around responding, explaining, and waiting, and now there was nothing, no emails, no follow-ups, no looming deadlines, just a short notice confirming that the review was closed with limited adjustments and no further action required. At first the relief was overwhelming, a physical release he had not realized he was holding in his body, yet as days passed that relief slowly transformed into unease, because Michael knew that while the audit was over, the systems that had initiated it were still watching, still learning, still updating their perception of his business based on everything that had just occurred. His logistics firm had survived, but survival alone did not feel like victory, not after the toll the process had taken on his team, his confidence, and his appetite for risk, and for the first time since becoming an entrepreneur he found himself questioning whether growth was worth the invisible costs of attention. It was during this period of uncertainty that his compliance director suggested something that initially sounded counterintuitive: instead of trying to forget the audit, they should study it, dissect it, and feed it back into the AI compliance system that had supported them throughout the process, turning every interaction into data rather than trauma. Slowly, methodically, they uploaded correspondence, requests, responses, timelines, and outcomes, allowing the system to reconstruct the audit from start to finish, identifying patterns that no one had noticed in real time, such as how certain explanations shortened response cycles while others invited deeper questioning, and how specific financial ratios consistently attracted attention even when ultimately accepted. Watching the analysis unfold was unsettling but empowering for Michael, because it reframed the audit as something intelligible rather than arbitrary, revealing that the investigation had followed a logic shaped by algorithms and historical precedent rather than hostility or suspicion, and that logic could be learned. As weeks turned into months the AI began suggesting subtle changes, recommending adjustments to reporting cadence, documentation depth, and decision timing that would reduce the likelihood of similar scrutiny in the future, not by shrinking the business but by smoothing its data profile and reinforcing narrative consistency across years. Gradually Michael's fear gave way to confidence, because instead of guessing whether the next decision might trigger attention, he could see how it fit into a broader risk trajectory informed by real outcomes rather than assumptions. The true transformation came a year later when his company filed its next return, a moment that would once have filled him with dread, yet this time felt almost routine, as the AI confirmed alignment, flagged no major concerns, and projected a significantly lower audit probability than before, reflecting a system that had absorbed the lessons of the past and adjusted accordingly. Sitting alone in his office after submitting the filing, Michael realized that the audit had not marked the end of his company's freedom but the beginning of a new maturity, one where uncertainty was replaced by understanding and fear by preparation, because the silence that followed was no longer empty, it was filled with quiet confidence, the knowledge that even if the questions returned someday, his business would not face them blindly again, having learned how to listen, adapt, and grow stronger in a world where being observed was no longer an exception but the rule.

Chapter 10

The Invisible Advantage: Designing a Business That Algorithms Leave Alone

In the final analysis the highest form of audit defense is not a tactic, a tool, or even a system, but an outcome, the quiet and powerful state in which a business becomes so internally coherent, externally consistent, and statistically predictable that enforcement algorithms deprioritize it entirely, moving on to targets that promise a higher return on investigative effort, and achieving this invisible advantage requires understanding how modern regulatory systems think, what they value, and how they allocate attention in a world where resources are finite but data is infinite. Artificial intelligence has fundamentally changed enforcement by replacing suspicion with probability, meaning that businesses are no longer judged by isolated actions but by their overall behavioral profile across time, entities, and contexts, and those profiles that consistently align with expectations are quietly categorized as low yield, making them less likely to be selected for audits, reviews, or extended inquiries. Designing a business that algorithms leave alone therefore becomes a strategic discipline, one that blends AI-driven analytics with intentional governance, standardized execution, and long-term narrative consistency, ensuring that every financial signal reinforces trust rather than uncertainty. This does not mean avoiding innovation, complexity, or aggressive growth, but rather managing them in ways that remain legible to machines, smoothing transitions, documenting intent, and aligning reporting structures so that change appears deliberate rather than erratic. AI plays a central role in this process by continuously modeling how the business appears from the outside, monitoring risk trajectories, and highlighting deviations before they harden into patterns, allowing leadership teams to course-correct subtly and proactively rather than react dramatically after attention has already been triggered. Over time this creates a compounding effect, where each clean filing, each consistent explanation, and each resolved inquiry strengthens the business's credibility profile, gradually lowering its priority in enforcement queues and reducing the likelihood that human investigators will ever become involved. Importantly this invisible advantage extends beyond tax authorities, influencing how banks, investors, insurers, and partners assess risk, because many of these institutions now rely on similar data-driven models to evaluate stability and trustworthiness, meaning that a business optimized for algorithmic credibility enjoys broader benefits across the financial ecosystem. Achieving this state requires a shift in mindset, moving away from seeing compliance as something that happens to the business and toward treating it as something the business actively designs, embedding AI into planning, execution, and review processes so that every decision contributes to a coherent, defensible story that remains consistent even as the company evolves. By the end of this chapter you will understand how to integrate the lessons of this book into a unified approach that transforms audit defense from a reactive necessity into a quiet strategic edge, allowing your business to operate confidently, grow intelligently, and remain largely invisible to the systems designed to find problems, not because there is nothing happening, but because everything happening makes sense.

"The Quiet File"

No one noticed when the file stopped moving, not at first, because in a system built to track millions of businesses simultaneously, attention is measured in motion, flags, escalations, and queues, and when a company's data settles into predictable rhythms it simply drifts downward in priority until it becomes background noise, a quiet file among thousands of others, and that was exactly what happened to the company Alex Morgan built, though he would not understand the significance of it until years later. Alex had founded his software services firm with ambition but not bravado, scaling carefully, making deliberate choices, and investing early in systems that brought order to complexity, not because he feared audits, but because he believed clarity created freedom, and over time that belief shaped how the business operated in ways that were subtle but profound. Every expansion was phased, every restructuring documented, every reporting change aligned with prior narratives, and while none of this felt dramatic in the moment, it created a data history that unfolded smoothly year after year, telling a story of steady evolution rather than abrupt transformation. Behind the scenes AI systems monitored this history continuously, recalculating risk scores, comparing patterns, and quietly updating Alex's company's profile, and with each passing year the indicators trended downward, not because activity slowed, but because variability decreased, explanations remained consistent, and anomalies were addressed before they became patterns. Alex never received a letter, never faced an investigation, and never experienced the disruption so many peers described, which initially felt like luck, until one evening at a conference when a former regulator mentioned casually that their agency's systems were designed to ignore businesses whose data histories suggested low probability of error or abuse, because time and resources were better spent elsewhere. That comment lingered in Alex's mind, prompting him to review his company's compliance dashboards with new curiosity, and what he saw surprised him, a long, unbroken record of alignment, consistency, and responsiveness that had effectively rendered the company uninteresting to enforcement algorithms, a status more valuable than any single deduction or short-term tax strategy. Years later when Alex sold the business the due diligence process unfolded with remarkable ease, as automated risk assessments cleared instantly, documentation aligned perfectly, and reviewers found no unresolved questions, leading one advisor to remark that the company was unusually "clean," a word that carried more weight than Alex realized at the time. Reflecting on the journey after the sale, Alex understood that the greatest advantage he had built was not a product or a market position, but an invisible reputation encoded in data, a quiet file that never needed attention because it never gave the systems watching it a reason to look twice, and in a world increasingly governed by algorithms, that quiet was the loudest signal of all.

Final Thoughts

Building a Business That Can Withstand the Future

In a world where artificial intelligence increasingly governs how businesses are evaluated, monitored, and selected for scrutiny, the concept of audit defense has evolved far beyond preparation and response, becoming instead a matter of design, intention, and long-term coherence, because modern enforcement systems do not merely examine isolated events but observe behavior over time, learning which companies demonstrate clarity, consistency, and credibility and which ones appear chaotic, contradictory, or statistically abnormal. Throughout this book you have seen that audits are no longer driven primarily by human suspicion or randomness but by probability models that continuously assess risk based on data patterns, meaning that every transaction, classification, and reporting decision quietly contributes to a cumulative profile that determines whether a business becomes a target or remains invisible. This reality may feel unsettling at first, but it also presents an extraordinary opportunity, because the same intelligence that creates risk can be harnessed to eliminate it, transforming compliance from a reactive obligation into a proactive strategic advantage. The businesses that thrive in this environment are not those that hide or avoid complexity, but those that structure complexity intelligently, using AI to ensure that growth, innovation, and optimization unfold in ways that remain legible and defensible to the systems that observe them. As you have learned, audit defense begins long before an inquiry ever arrives, through AI-driven risk scoring, digital audit trails, real-time monitoring, and defensible decision-making frameworks that align human judgment with machine expectations. These tools do more than protect against penalties or investigations; they fundamentally improve how businesses operate, bringing clarity to financial narratives, discipline to strategic choices, and confidence to leadership teams navigating an increasingly regulated and data-driven economy. Importantly, this approach does not require sacrificing profitability or ambition, but rather integrating compliance intelligence into the fabric of operations so that every gain is sustainable and every advantage is protected. The stories in this book illustrate a powerful truth: businesses that embrace AI-guided compliance do not merely survive audits, they outgrow them, gradually becoming low-priority entities in enforcement systems that are designed to pursue uncertainty rather than order. Over time this creates what can best be described as audit immunity—not the absence of oversight, but the presence of trust encoded in data, consistency, and history. As you move forward, the goal is not perfection but coherence, not fear but understanding, and not resistance to AI but mastery of it, because in a future where algorithms decide where attention flows, the most powerful position is to become uninteresting for all the right reasons. By applying the principles in this book you are not simply protecting your business from today's audits, you are future-proofing it for a regulatory landscape that will only become more automated, more analytical, and more unforgiving of disorder, ensuring that your company remains resilient, credible, and confidently positioned to grow under constant observation.

www.ingramcontent.com/pod-product-compliance
Lightning Source LLC
LaVergne TN
LVHW022026200926
848481LV00007B/2558